MW01441462

A PROVERBS 31 WARRIOR'S CREED

50 DEVOTIONS TO ELEVATE YOUR SPIRITUAL INTELLIGENCE AND WIN THE FIGHT FOR YOUR FAMILY

Dr. Temi Michael-O

Foreword by Dawn Collis

Unless otherwise stated, Bible quotations are taken from the Holy Bible, King James Version (KJV), Public Domain.

Scripture taken from the New King James Version®. Copyright © 1982 by Thomas Nelson. Used by permission. All rights reserved.

Scripture quotations marked (NIV) are taken from the Holy Bible, New International Version®, NIV®. Copyright © 1973, 1978, 1984, 2011 by Biblica, Inc.™ Used by permission of Zondervan.

Scripture quotations marked (AMP) are taken from the AMPLIFIED® BIBLE, Copyright© 1954, 1958, 1962, 1964, 1965, 1987 by the Lockman Foundation Used by Permission. (www.Lockman.org)

Scripture quotations are taken from the Holy Bible, New Living Translation, copyright ©1996, 2004, 2015 by Tyndale House Foundation. Used by permission of Tyndale House Publishers, Carol Stream, Illinois 60188. All rights reserved.

Scripture quotations taken from the (NASB®) New American Standard Bible®, Copyright © 1995 by The Lockman Foundation. Used by permission. All rights reserved. lockman.org

JPS Tanakh Copyrighted © 1985 by The Jewish Publication Society, which owns worldwide rights to Tanakh: The Holy Scriptures.

Copyright © 2024 by Temitope Olaniran
Published By: Habakkuk 2vs2
ISBN: 979-8-9918543-3-7
Library of Congress Control Number: 2024927562

For more information:
www.littleonespiecmh.com
www.christianmommas.com

Table of Contents

ACKNOWLEDGMENTS v
FOREWORD vii
INTRODUCTION. ix
DAY 1. 1
DAY 2. 5
DAY 3. 9
DAY 4. 14
DAY 5. 17
DAY 6. 21
DAY 7. 25
DAY 8. 29
DAY 9. 33
DAY 10. 37
DAY 11. 41
DAY 12. 45
DAY 13. 49
DAY 14. 53
DAY 15. 57
DAY 16. 61
DAY 17. 65
DAY 18. 70
DAY 19. 74
DAY 20. 78
DAY 21. 82
DAY 22. 86
DAY 23. 91
DAY 24. 95

DAY 25	99
DAY 26	103
DAY 27	106
DAY 28	110
DAY 29	115
DAY 30	120
DAY 31	124
DAY 32	129
DAY 33	134
DAY 34	139
DAY 35	143
DAY 36	148
DAY 37	153
DAY 38	157
DAY 39	160
DAY 40	165
DAY 41	170
DAY 42	174
DAY 43	179
DAY 44	184
DAY 45	189
DAY 46	194
DAY 47	198
DAY 48	202
DAY 49	206
DAY 50	210
ABOUT ME	216

Acknowledgments

All Glory to God who teaches my hands to war and my fingers to fight. I am thankful for the help of the Holy Spirit, the Spirit of revelation, wisdom, and understanding.

Special thanks to my husband and man of valor, Michael Olaniran, for his support.

To my mighty men of valor, Josef, Josiah, and Joel, thinking of your future motivates me. I am thankful God sent you to me.

Special thanks you to Pastors Mirek and Linda Hufton of World Harvest Church, Roswell, Georgia, for guiding me to follow the Word and the Spirit.

To the Proverbs 31 warrior holding this book, thank you for choosing to fight for your family and access the spiritual intel you need to manifest your true identity. Together, we are taking territories for God's kingdom!

Foreword

Do you see yourself as a warrior, fighting for your family and the kingdom of God?

It is both an honor and a joy to write the foreword for this life-transforming book! Having studied Proverbs 31 many times, I've drawn wisdom from it to apply to my life. Yet, Temi brings a fresh perspective in these pages. Like the sons of Issachar, she understands the times and knows what we must do. As women, we are warriors for our families. Satan would love nothing more than to destroy the family unit. Temi shows you how to win the war for your family and the kingdom of God.

She practices the principles of the Proverbs 31 woman. Several years ago, over Sunday prayer at church, I found myself drawn to her peaceful, joyful, and loving confidence. Reflecting on her prayer requests, I sensed an image of Temi's spirit that sets her apart. She, like David, has a heart after God's own heart. Her heart beats with God's love for others, as evidenced in her endless acts of service.

In my 64th year of marriage to the wonderful man God sent me, Glenn, and having four children (two daughters and their husbands), I recognize that we must always keep learning. There are new ways to see and utilize eternal principles. For example, the readings on days 7 and 8 (Proverbs 31:10-11) talk about trust. I learned the number one thing I must do – I must ground my identity in my relationship with God. THEN, I can expand my capacity to be a place of safety and comfort for my spouse. I can receive intel from the Lord on behalf of my husband and family.

In a world obsessed with temporal challenges, will you, as His warrior, accept an eternal challenge to defend, protect,and promote your family to the height God intended? As His warrior, using the tools Temi presents, you can experience total victory in every area. Simply press the principles she teaches into action.

As a Proverbs 31 warrior, you are a…
Woman of God,
Armed with His Word,
Resolute in Spirit,
Ready for Battle,
In step with the Lord,
On guard against the enemy, and
Resting in Him.
Are you up for the challenge? Let's go!

Dawn M. Collis
Associate Pastor, World Harvest Church, Roswell, GA.

Introduction

In 2022, I embarked on a transformative journey, exploring the life of the woman of valor depicted in Proverbs 31. Guided by the greatest teacher of truth, the Holy Spirit, my understanding of Proverbs 31:10-31 deepened. This journey became an experiential knowledge as I underwent deliverance from spiritual forces and mindsets that were hindering my progress. I learned, and continue to learn, how to be a woman of valor—training my spirit, exercising spiritual authority, and claiming victory over negative generational patterns.

Everything I have written in this book has been learned through the help of the Holy Spirit, and He will help you too as you invite Him into your daily journey.

Start by saying: "Holy Spirit, my name is [insert your name]. I acknowledge You as my helper. Help me journey through this book and transform me."

As a U.S. Army veteran, I have firsthand experience with the profound benefits of consistently reciting a creed. It is a meditative practice that has the power to retrain the subconscious mind and align your reality with the words you speak. Over the next 50 days, I encourage you to be intentional about boldly declaring the Proverbs 31 Warrior's Creed each day, visualizing your words in action. Inspired by Proverbs 31:10-31, this creed speaks Spirit and life, bringing you into covenant with God's Word. As you engage fully with the content of this book, anticipate a deepening intimacy with the Holy Spirit, a reprogramming of your subconscious mind, enriched family relationships, and more.

PROVERBS 31 WARRIOR'S CREED

I am a Woman of Valor under the command of the Lord of Hosts

I am blood bought, blood cleansed, and priced above rubies

I am under God's covering

I am operating with the wisdom from above

I am spiritually alert with a high level of sensitivity to my household's needs

I am kingdom-minded and make spiritual investments

I am a wise-hearted student of the Word, rightly dividing the Word of truth

I am a cheerful giver endued with the giving grace

I am covered by the blood of Jesus together with every member of my household

I am a royal priest and I wear God's glory

I am a minister of the gospel administering my gifts for the profit of all

I am laughing at days to come

I am a wise woman, speaking life and unveiling deep mysteries

I am a place of safety for my spouse

I serve my spouse and do him good all the days of my life

I am married to a man of spiritual intelligence and earthly influence

I am fully present for my household, purposeful, and diligent with family affairs

My children and husband arise and call me blessed. My husband also praises me

I am a woman who fears the Lord

I am eating the fruit of righteousness and labor of love for my household.

I am limitless, the gates are lifted before me here on earth and in the realms of the spirit

DAY 1

The words of king Lemuel, the prophecy that his mother taught him.

Proverbs 31:1 (KJV)

Today, I invite you to let go of the idea that the woman described in Proverbs 31 is a figment of a man's imagination. Yes, a king wrote Proverbs 31. However, the king's mother's prophetic teachings influenced his writing. Proverbs 31:1 (KJV) says, *The words of king Lemuel,* **the prophecy that his mother taught him.** The king wrote under the influence of the same Spirit that inspired his mother to sow some prophetic seeds into the soil of his heart. What a powerful and prophetic influence! Lay your hands on your womb/lower abdomen and prophesy: "My biological and spiritual children live under the influence of the Holy Spirit. They prophesy, see visions, and invent to transform the world and advance God's kingdom."

In the Old Testament, most kings were warriors (2 Samuel 11:1) because it takes the mindset of a warrior to gain and keep their kingdom or territories. In shaping the mind of a warrior king, the queen mother in Proverbs 31 intentionally taught her son to find a woman of valor. Women of valor raise warriors, preserving subsequent generations of valiant warriors.

Like the Queen Mother, parents must think and act like warriors. From the early years of life, we must train the spirit, soul, and body of the kings and queens under our care to embrace truth, resist darkness, discern relationships, and enforce victory over the battles of life.

Intel/Prophetic Insights

DAY 2

The words of king Lemuel, the prophecy that his mother taught him.

Proverbs 31:1 (KJV)

Because we live in a time of great confusion about the purpose and power of marriage, let us pause and digest some marriage truths by meditating on marriage truth in the Bible. Meditate by doing one of the following:

- Read each scripture slowly and several times after inviting the Holy Spirit to teach you. Then be still and listen for what the Holy Spirit is saying.

- Pray in the spirit while holding the scripture for meditation in mind. Let your mind focus on gaining a deeper understanding of the Bible verses. Then be still and listen for what the Holy Spirit is saying

And Adam said: "This is now bone of my bones And flesh of my flesh; She shall be called Woman, Because she was taken out of Man." Therefore *a man shall leave his father and mother and be joined to his wife, and they shall **become one** flesh.* **Genesis 2:23-24 (NKJV)**

*And He (Jesus) answered and said to them, "Have you not read that He who made them at the beginning 'made them male and female,' and said, 'For this reason a man shall leave his father and mother and be joined to his wife, and **the two shall become one flesh'?** So then, they are no longer two but one flesh. Therefore what God has joined together, let not man separate.* **Matthew 19:4-6 (NKJV)**

*But did He not **make them one**, Having a remnant of the Spirit? And why one? He seeks godly offspring. Therefore take heed to your spirit, And let none deal treacherously with the wife of his youth.* **Malachi 2:15 (NKJV)**

Intel/Prophetic Insights

DAY 3

A woman of valour who can find? For her price is far above rubies.

Proverbs 31:10 (JPS Tanakh)

Proverbs 31:10 reveals what should be the core of our identity—what makes us valuable and what should give us a positive sense of self. Your ability to establish or manifest God's will for your life and His purpose for your household depends on the depth of consciousness regarding your spiritual identity presented in Proverbs 31:10.

Knowing whose we are (who owns us) and who we are in the spirit realm shapes our earthly realities. That's why the enemy aims to skew our understanding or perception of our identity.

Similar to the Jewish culture exemplified in Genesis 24:53, it is common practice for grooms to pay brideprice in Nigeria, West Africa, where I was born. The bride's family would provide a list of things for the groom's family to purchase as evidence that they value the future wife and demonstrate the capacity to meet all her needs. They bring cows, fruits, money, clothes, and more. If it is on the list, the groom's family must search the universe and get it. ***What we pay and the sacrifices involved in procuring an item indicate its value.***

In Proverbs 31 verse 10, the price of a virtuous woman is far above rubies because she is first in a covenant relationship with her maker, who is her husband (Isaiah 54:5). Your Maker, the Lord of Hosts, paid a price above rubies—the Blood of Jesus—to receive you into His family.

As a Proverbs 31 warrior, the price Jesus paid with His blood gives you value and identity.

The blood of Jesus is your value. Jesus laid down His life to give you life. Your soul is precious to God. See it in the name of Jesus!

You are not worthless. People may have dishonored or called you worthless, but you aren't. We must live life with our worth or identity in Christ in mind. It changes our sense of self and how we treat others.

Taking Holy Communion often helps me remember my covenant relationship with Jesus and grounds me in the truth that the greatest price was paid for me to have eternal life. I invite you to take the Holy Communion often (Mark 14:22-25; John 6:56; 1 Corinthians 11:23-26).

*For I have received of the Lord that which also I delivered unto you, That the Lord Jesus the same night in which he was betrayed took bread: And when he had given thanks, he brake it, and said, Take, eat: this is my body, which is broken for you: **this do in remembrance of me**. After* *the same manner also he took the cup, when he had supped, saying, This cup is the new testament in my blood: this do ye, as oft as ye drink it, in remembrance of me. For **as often** as ye eat this bread, and drink this cup, ye do shew the Lord's death till he come.*

1 Corinthians 11:23-26 (KJV)

Intel/Prophetic Insights

DAY 4

For your husband is your Maker, Whose name is the LORD of armies; And your Redeemer is the Holy One of Israel, Who is called the God of all the earth.

Isaiah 54:5 (NASB)

Meditate on Isaiah 54:5 by doing one of the following:

- Read the Bible verse personalized several times after inviting the Holy Spirit to teach you. Then be still and listen for what the Holy Spirit is saying.

- Pray in the spirit while holding Isaiah 54:5 in mind. Let your mind focus on gaining a deeper understanding of the Bible verse. Then be still and listen for what the Holy Spirit is saying.

- Pray in the spirit while declaring Isaiah 54:5 personalized. Then be still and listen for what the Holy Spirit is saying.

Intel/Prophetic Insights

DAY 5

A woman of valour who can find? For her price is far above rubies.

Proverbs 31:10 (JPS Tanakh)

The Jewish Publication Society translation of **Proverbs 31:10** says, *A woman of valour who can find? For her price is far above rubies.* Valour is associated with warfare and courage, and the warrior nature of a Proverbs 31 woman is evident in the use of her hands and arms (Proverbs 31:13, 16, 17, 19, 20, 31). It takes a warfare mindset and courage to overcome the challenges associated with family life and other aspects of life that intersect the family ecosystem.

King David, One of the greatest warriors in the Bible, declares in **Psalm 18:34 (NKJV)**, *He teaches my hands to make war, So that my arms can bend a bow of bronze.* In **Psalm 144:1 (NKJV)**, he declares, *Blessed be the LORD my Rock, Who trains my hands for war, And my fingers for battle.*

A Proverbs 31 woman is tagged a valor because of her price. She entered the ranks of the more than conquerors because Jesus, the Lord of Hosts, paid a price for her to join his family and receive the Holy

Spirit, a spiritual inheritance that powers the more than conquerors life. The Amplified version of **Romans 8:37** declares, *Yet in all these things we are more than conquerors and gain an overwhelming victory through Him who loved us [so much that He died for us].* With this in mind, A Proverbs 31 warrior only fights to enforce victory. From this moment you will fight secured in the love of the one who defeated satan, your greatest foe. In Jesus's name. Amen.

Declare this truth at least 100 times today: I AM MORE THAN A CONQUEROR THROUGH JESUS CHRIST.

Intel/Prophetic Insights

DAY 6

A woman of valour who can find? For her price is far above rubies.

Proverbs 31:10 (JPS Tanakh)

In response to the one who disarmed principalities and powers for her and gave her authority over them (Colossians 2:15), a Proverbs 31 woman enlists as a soldier for Christ, taking orders from Him and living under His covering. As we mature in the understanding of the finished works of Jesus and the consequences of losing covering, we will subjugate the fear of man and become a force to reckon with in the spiritual and physical realms.

The consciousness of Jesus as a husband who is the Lord of Hosts or the God of angel armies in command of our lives and one who protects those on his side (Isaiah 54:5; Joshua 5:13-15; Romans 8:31) empowers me to submit to the Lordship of Jesus and resist any expression of darkness in my realm.

The book of instructions approved by my commander, the Holy Bible, is the final authority in my marital decisions, parenting choices, and other aspects of life. It doesn't matter how hard or foolish it seems to the natural mind, I am determined to choose obedience consistently. It does not matter what strangers, acquaintances, or loved ones think about a matter, I live to please the one who protects my household and provides for us.

Consistently reflect on your parenting, marriage, career, and so on, and ask the Holy Spirit to help you see if your practices in those areas of your life are driven by the fear of God or the fear of man.

You therefore must endure hardship as a good soldier of Jesus Christ. No one engaged in warfare entangles himself with the affairs of this life, that he may please him who enlisted him as a soldier. **2 Timothy 2:3-4 (NKJV)**

Intel/Prophetic Insights

DAY 7

The heart of her husband doth safely trust in her, so that he shall have no need of spoil.

Proverbs 31:11 (KJV)

What happens when the hearts of a couple safely trust in each other? One becomes a place of safety and comfort for the other. For example, the husband will always be vulnerable with his wife, guarding the marriage against adultery (physical and emotional). When tempted or struggling with lustful thoughts, he will most likely be vulnerable enough to communicate his experiences, seek accountability, and allow his wife to enforce victory with him in prayer.

Therefore, ***confess your sins to one another, and pray for one another so that you may be healed****. A prayer of a righteous person, when it is brought about, can accomplish much.* **James 5:16 (NASB)**

Prayer and vulnerability are crucial for establishing healing from internal wounds responsible for sins that cause friction in marital relationships.

Reflect: What does trust mean to you? How often does your spouse share his weaknesses or temptations with you? And how do you usually respond to your spouse? Do you fight your spouse or fight alongside your spouse to overcome weaknesses or temptations?

Intel/Prophetic Insights

DAY 8

The heart of her husband doth safely trust in her, so that he shall have no need of spoil.

Proverbs 31:11 (KJV)

As you ground your identity in your relationship with God (Proverbs 31:10), you expand your capacity to be a place of safety and comfort for your spouse. We can't be a place of safety for anyone if our hearts are not constantly guided and guarded to trust in God. We can only give comfort if we have an established relationship with the God of All Comfort (2 Corinthians 1:3-4).

A Proverbs 31 warrior is a place of safety for her husband because she is under the command of the Lord of Hosts, positioning her to receive spiritual intel from God on behalf of her family. Hence, she can see the danger lurking around her spouse, warn him, intercede, and provide godly wisdom for navigating challenging situations.

As you receive spiritual intel from God about your spouse and bear the fruit of the Spirit through intimacy with the Holy Spirit, your spouse will find safety in your relationship and have no need of spoil. Some spirits drive husbands to need spoil, to covet things, or other women. There are generational curses that make husbands blind to the good in their wives. It takes spiritual intelligence to break the stronghold of those curses.

One of my testimonies is freedom from demonic sexual molestation. For about five years of my marriage life, demons sexually molested me in my sleep due to demonic covenants and occult practices in my natural bloodline. Furthermore, past sins opened the door to demonic oppression. Until I stopped the psychoanalysis of my problems and began to build intimacy with the Holy Spirit, I couldn't walk in freedom, nor could I use spiritual intel to help my spouse enforce victory over life's challenges. My marriage experienced a turnaround when yielding to the Holy Spirit became my norm. I began to see the Lord of Hosts as my husband and developed a new sense of identity.

Yes, you can become a place of safety for your spouse and help him walk in freedom. Let the Lord of Hosts become your commander and yield to His Spirit. Wake up to pray and fast when summoned, forgive quickly, and obey the Word every season. You can do all things through Christ, which strengthens you!

Imagine and Declare this with all your heart: THE HEART OF MY HUSBAND SAFELY TRUSTS IN ME.

Intel/Prophetic Insights

DAY 9

The heart of her husband doth safely trust in her, so that he shall have no need of spoil.

Proverbs 31:11 (KJV)

We feel safe around people who communicate our love language. For example, if receiving words of affirmation is one of your primary ways of receiving love, you will feel secure in relationships where words of affirmation are consistently communicated, creating an atmosphere of vulnerability. The Bible has revealed that "respect" is an essential love language for men in marriage. **Ephesians 5:33 (NKJV)** declares, *Nevertheless let each one of you in particular so love his own wife as himself, and let the wife see that she respects her husband.*

As Proverbs 31 women, we must lean on God's wisdom in marriage. If His Word instructs us to respect our husbands, it is for our good. We should see God's instruction in Ephesians 5:22-33 as guidance for strengthening our marital relationship. Giving respect is a crucial seed we sow to create a physically and emotionally safe space in marriage.

Giving respect to one's husband may be difficult when trust has been broken or when one lacks role models. Whatever the case, God understands, and the Holy Spirit is available to help us. The Helper can assist you in truly being a help-meet for your spouse, meeting your husband's need for respect (John 14:26; Genesis 2:18). Jesus said, *But the Helper, the Holy Spirit, whom the Father will send in My name, He will teach you all things, and bring to your remembrance all things that I said to you.* **John 14:26 (NKJV)**

For me, respecting my husband means speaking well of him at all times, correcting him privately after seeking God's help, not pointing out or discussing his mistakes in public, seeking his input when making major decisions, and not competing for leadership in the home. Due to my upbringing, it took the great help of the Holy Spirit to learn these things. The Holy Spirit is available to help you as well. If married, consider asking your husband what having respect for one's husband looks like. Ask God to help you see couples modeling Ephesians 5:33 around you, then spend quality time with them.

Say this, then pray in the Spirit: Holy Spirit, I accept You as my Helper in marriage. I need Your help. Teach me how to respect my husband.

Intel/Prophetic Insights

DAY 10

She will do him good and not evil all the days of her life.

Proverbs 31:12 (KJV)

A Proverbs 31 woman does her husband good all the days of her life because she serves the Good God and bears his nature of goodness (Psalm 25:8; Psalm 31: 19-20; Psalm 34:8; Psalm 143:10; Psalm 119:68; Nahum 1:7).

Doing our husbands good encompasses caring for their spirit, soul, and body. Because supporting the spiritual development of an individual intersects their physical and soul care, we will primarily focus on doing good to a spouse's spirit.

What God considers "good" differs from what the world teaches and our natural perception of good. Consider the following exhortation in **1 Timothy 2:1-4**: *I exhort therefore, that, first of all, supplications, prayers, intercessions, and giving of thanks, be made for all men; For kings, and for all that are in authority; that we may lead a quiet and peaceable life in all godliness and honesty. For this is good and acceptable* *in the sight of God our Saviour; Who will have all men to be saved, and to come unto the knowledge of the truth.*

Reflect: Assess your understanding of goodness from a spiritual and emotional perspective. What good things can you continue or begin to do to support your spouse?

Intel/Prophetic Insights

DAY 11

She will do him good and not evil all the days of her life.

Proverbs 31:12 (KJV)

1 Timothy 2:1-4 highlights some "good things" we do not often think of—supplication, prayer, intercession, and giving thanks. Often, meeting the physical needs of others comes to mind when we think of doing "good things." Rightly so, it is good to meet physical needs in marriage. Yet, we can do the greatest good by supporting spiritual growth through supplications, prayers, intercessions, and giving thanks so that godliness and honesty can become a culture in the home.

The good you want to see in your spouse is dependent on the spiritual investments of good you make for him. You can never go wrong praying for your husband's spiritual growth.

You ask [God for something] and do not receive it, because you ask with wrong motives [out of selfishness or with an unrighteous agenda], so that [when you get what you want] you may spend it on your [hedonistic] desires. **James 4:3 (AMP)**

A passionate desire to see God glorified in our spouses' lives must be the driving force behind our prayers for them. If the goal is to brag about our spouse, get our spouse to do what pleases us, or so we can brag about the spiritual investments we are making to see their lives transformed, we hinder the effectiveness of our prayers.

Imagine and Declare this with all your heart: I DO MY HUSBAND GOOD ALL THE DAYS OF MY LIFE

Intel/Prophetic Insights

DAY 12

She will do him good and not evil all the days of her life.

Proverbs 31:12 (KJV)

Pray fervently that your spouse will grow deeper in love with God, love righteousness and hate wickedness, and become a man after God's heart. Send angels to align your spouse with divine relationships and separate your spouse from relationships sabotaging their spiritual growth. Consider fasting and praying to receive strategies to help your spouse overcome a pattern of spiritual growth followed by spiritual laxity or stagnation. Set your spouse on fire with Holy Spirit-inspired prayers. Pray in tongues. Give thanks for past victories, the progress you notice, and the future you desire for your spouse.

Prayer: Heavenly Father, in the name of Jesus and by the power in the blood of Jesus, deliver my husband from self-destructive behaviors and generational curses. Teach my husband to love himself the way you want him to and to love you above all else so he can live for you and fulfill your will for our marriage. In the name of Jesus, I decree and declare victory over every foundational issue that hinders my husband from becoming one with me. From this moment, I operate in divine wisdom in my marriage and enjoy God's will of peace and unity in my home. Thank you, Jesus!

Intel/Prophetic Insights

DAY 13

She will do him good and not evil all the days of her life.

Proverbs 31:12 (KJV)

If married with children, supporting fathering is an important way to do your husband good.

Engage your spiritual weapons to solve problems such as negative fathering patterns that disrupt healthy father-child relationships. With spiritual intelligence, we will win arguments with words of wisdom and prayer, guiding the house in a direction that pleases God.

I will therefore that the younger women marry, bear children, ***guide the house****, give none occasion to the adversary to speak reproachfully.* **1 Timothy 5:14 (KJV)**

Connection with Positive Role Models

Studies show that fathers experience hormonal and psychological changes when transitioning to fatherhood. The physiological and psychological changes fathers experience often enhance their capacity to nurture their children. The concept of fatherhood constellation suggests that fatherhood changes men and stirs the need for father figures, the need for a relationship with other fathers, and a connection with one's father. Since fatherhood awakens these good desires, it means helping fathers actualize the desire for relationships with other fathers can yield positive outcomes.

With that said, we can support fathers by guiding them to relationships that can strengthen father-child relationships. Mommas, this is where spiritual discernment and wisdom are key. Let's observe the values of father figures around us and engage spiritual judgment to guide our children's fathers to relationships that align with our faith values, particularly Biblical beliefs about parenting and marriage.

Proverbs 13:20 (AMP) *says, He who walks [as a companion] with wise men will be wise, But the companions of [conceited, dull-witted] fools [are fools themselves and] will experience harm.* Let's connect fathers with wise men and expect the wise association to have a positive influence on their fathering.

Ask God for wisdom to strengthen father-child relationships and ask your spouse. Consider saying, "I want to strengthen your relationship with our children. Do you have any suggestions on how to do this?"

Intel/Prophetic Insights

DAY 14

Her husband is known in the gates, When he sits among the elders of the land.

Proverbs 31:23 (NKJV)

Gates represent places of influence, decision-making, and access to vital intelligence (Consider Ruth 4:1-12). The word "elders" is synonymous with decision-makers, authority figures, or influencers. A man who can access spiritual gates will be known in the earthly gates. A Proverbs 31 warrior's husband is known in the gates because her spiritual adventures positively impact her spouse. We can make our spouses become known in the gates by guiding them to prioritize their spiritual growth. Have a marriage altar sustained by spiritual (and sexual) intimacy with your spouse. Sexual intimacy promotes sexual purity in marriage (1 Corinthians 7:5) and prevents spiritual defilement, thereby keeping the fire on the personal, marriage, and household altar burning. Spiritual disciplines such as fasting, praying, vigils, meditation, Word study, and so on should be engaged jointly as much as possible. This is an important way for husbands and wives to become forces to reckon with in the gates.

Our spouses cannot become victims of decisions made by earthly decision-makers on their jobs or in the government if they are among the elders, spiritually, socially, and economically. Encourage your spouse to serve God instead of competing with him, and doing so will make him a role model to your children and society.

Imagine and Declare this with all your heart: I **AM MARRIED TO A MAN OF SPIRITUAL INTELLIGENCE AND EARTHLY INFLUENCE. MY HUSBAND IS KNOWN IN THE GATES. MY HUSBAND MAKES WISE DECISIONS.**

Intel/Prophetic Insights

DAY 15

***She seeketh wool, and flax**, and worketh willingly with her hands.*

Proverbs 31:13 (KJV)

The word **seek** implies deliberate, strategic, and continuous searching, and in God's kingdom, seekers always find (Matthew 7:8). We are called to "a life of seeking" in God's kingdom (Jeremiah 29:13; Matthew 6:33; Psalm 27:8; 2 Chronicles 7:14). Seeking demonstrates spiritual intelligence, and it positions us to receive or download spiritual intelligence. We must not fall into the deception that we have arrived. When we stop seeking, we start living in a state of ignorance and spiritual laxity, leading to sin and the loss of spiritual covering. A Proverbs 31 warrior is intentional about seeking from the source.

Flax and wool are raw materials used for making clothes. Clothes cover our nakedness, reducing our vulnerability to the elements. Sin brings nakedness (Lamentations 1:8), and clothes became necessary to buffer us from the power of shame caused by sin (Genesis 2:25; Genesis 3:7, 10, 21).

To avoid shame and unobstructed exposure to the adverse spiritual weather conditions in the world or fiery darts of the enemy (lies, false ideologies, demonic oppressions), we must seek God's covering. We must seek and stay under God's covering to prevent the enemy from successfully infiltrating our homes.

As we grow in our understanding of God's grace and what sin seeks to do to the human soul and lineage, we will shun sin, quickly repenting when we fall short with a deep disdain for the wicked nature of sin.

Job and God's hedge of protection

Job's story reveals that being under God's covering places a hedge of protection around us and our households. **Job 1:1&10** says, *There was a man in the land of Uz, whose name was Job; and that man was blameless and upright, and one who* **feared God and shunned evil**. *Have You not* **made a hedge around him, around his household,** *and around all that he has on every side? You have blessed the work of his hands, and his possessions have increased in the land.* God is always looking for one person to stand in the gap and secure the hedge of protection (Ezekiel 13:5 & 22:30). **Your family's hedge of protection is connected to your relationship with God!**

Intel/Prophetic Insights

DAY 16

She seeketh wool, and flax, and worketh willingly with her hands.

Proverbs 31:13 (KJV)

Flax and Wool, Beyond Physical Clothing

Hosea 2:5 (KJV) says, *For their mother hath played the harlot: she that conceived them hath done shamefully: for she said, I will go after my lovers, that give me my bread and my water, my wool and my flax, mine oil and my drink.* And **Hosea 2:9 (KJV)** says, *Therefore will I return, and take away my corn in the time thereof, and my wine in the season thereof, and will recover my wool and my flax given to cover her nakedness.*

Comparing Proverbs 31:13 with Hosea 2:5 and 9, we can see that flax and wool go beyond physical clothing. Charm is deceptive, and beauty does not last; but a woman who fears the LORD will be greatly praised (Proverbs 31:30)—a Proverbs 31 warrior seeks the covering of God, her first love, the one who provides flax and wool. **Seeking to stay under God's covering is spiritual intelligence and a weapon against the deceitfulness of sin (Hebrews 3:13).**

In Hosea 2, God's people lost their covering when they relied on humans for help and adopted ungodly ways. With unbiblical views about the family system infiltrating the church and anti-Christ practices being imposed on us like never before, it is easy to be swayed and bow to the nature of sin, stepping outside our spiritual covering.

I have given in to a sinful lifestyle before and experienced the spiritual and mental torment caused by the loss of spiritual covering. Now, I am currently enjoying the benefits of choosing a life that keeps me under God's covering. While this requires a lot of sacrifices and daily crucifixion of the flesh, it is the best path. I urge you to remain under God's covering. Return to God wholeheartedly when you fall short.

I am learning to repent quickly and not to fall into the trap of offense, pride, gossiping, and other sins that seek to master me (Genesis 4:7). Whenever I fall into the trap of offense and justify my right to be offended, I experience spiritual attacks. My family bears the consequences as well. God will not break His Word—We cannot continue living in sin and flourish (Romans 6:1; Proverbs 28:13).

Intel/Prophetic Insights

DAY 17

***She seeketh wool, and flax,** and worketh willingly with her hands.*

Proverbs 31:13 (KJV)

We are most vulnerable outside God's covering—we open ourselves and our homes to shame, confusion, unnecessary heartaches, and spiritual battles that impede our capacity to manifest our divine identity.

Let's explore two crucial ways to remain under God's covering:

- We must **jealously guard our relationship with God** by growing in love with God and fearing Him. *The fear of the LORD is to hate evil: pride, and arrogancy, and the evil way (Proverbs 8:13). Let those who love the LORD hate evil, for he guards the lives of his faithful ones and delivers them from the hand of the wicked (Psalm 97:10).* Are you a faithful lover? Are you jealously guarding your relationship with God? Like David, may this be the cry of your heart, *"Search me, O God, and know my heart; Try me, and know my anxieties; And see if there is any* *wicked way in me, And lead me in the way everlasting." Psalm 139:23-24*

- We must **live dependent on God**, trusting His ways and capacity to meet ALL our needs. Isaiah 30:1-5 (KJV) declares: *Woe to the rebellious children, saith the LORD, that take counsel, but not of me; and that cover with a covering, but not of my spirit, that they may add sin to sin: that walk to go down into Egypt, and have not asked at my mouth; to strengthen themselves in the strength of Pharaoh, and to trust in the shadow of Egypt! Therefore shall the strength of Pharaoh be your shame, and the trust in the shadow of Egypt your confusion. For his princes were at Zoan, and his ambassadors came to Hanes. They were all ashamed of a people that could not profit them, nor be an help nor profit, but a shame, and also a reproach.*

Those who look to God will never be naked or ashamed (Psalm 25:3; 34:5). Our capacity to live dependent on God expands as we grow in our relationship with him. Investing time in prayer, Bible study, and meditation is essential for developing our relationship with God and remaining under God's covering. Jesus' life reveals that living dependent on God is powered by praying (Luke 5:16; Luke 6:12; Matthew 14:23; Mark 1:35) and learning the Word (Luke 2:46-49; Luke 4:16-21).

Like Jesus, we must practice praying all night, or rise early as the Spirit leads us to grow beyond knowing about God to knowing Him. Like Jesus, we must be that workman, studying God's word to access high-level spiritual illumination that breaks the strongholds of lust, pride, and other sins in our lives, and keeps us spiritually covered and free from shame (2 Timothy 2:15; 2 Corinthians 5:21; Matthew 26:41). As we know God, His fire will burn in us, destroying the desire for sin, allowing God's light in us to light up our household and spheres of influence.

Intel/Prophetic Insights

DAY 18

*She seeketh wool, and flax, and **worketh willingly with her hands**.*

Proverbs 31:13 (KJV)

She works willingly with her hands.

One of the greatest works we can do is to work out our salvation with fear and trembling, living righteously or choosing God's ways despite the cost, acknowledging that the almighty God is working in you both to will and to work for His good pleasure (Philippians 2:12-13).

We must be willing to fight the good fight of faith (1 Timothy 6:12).

Persecution is inevitable when we choose to embrace God's standard for our family life. Many will not understand us, and seasons of loneliness will arise. But if we are willing to work God's way, we will shield our family from unnecessary spiritual battles and heartaches.

Meditate on the scriptures below by doing one of the following:

- Read each scripture slowly and several times after inviting the Holy Spirit to teach you. Then be still and listen for what the Holy Spirit is saying.

- Pray in the spirit while holding the scripture for meditation in mind. Let your mind focus on gaining a deeper understanding of the Bible verses. Then be still and listen for what the Holy Spirit is saying.

1 John 3:10 (AMP)

By this the children of God and the children of the devil are clearly identified: anyone who does not practice righteousness [who does not seek God's will in thought, action, and purpose] is not of God, nor is the one who does not [unselfishly] love his [believing] brother.

Psalm 110:3 (AMP)

Your people will offer themselves willingly [to participate in Your battle] in the day of Your power; In the splendor of holiness, from the womb of the dawn, Your young men are to You as the dew.

Acts 10:35 (NKJV)

But in every nation whoever fears Him and works righteousness is accepted by Him.

1 John 3:7 (NKJV)

Little children, let no one deceive you. He who practices righteousness is righteous, just as He is righteous.

Intel/Prophetic Insights

DAY 19

She seeketh wool, and flax, ***and worketh willingly with her hands.***

Proverbs 31:13 (KJV)

We must willingly work righteousness. We must contend for righteousness to find expression through our lives.

Proverbs 14:34 (AMP)

Righteousness [moral and spiritual integrity and virtuous character] exalts a nation, But sin is a disgrace to any people.

Isaiah 32:17 (NKJV)

The work of righteousness will be peace, And the effect of righteousness, quietness and assurance forever.

Prayer: Heavenly Father, you are my lover, my husband, and my source. Your Word says, if we confess our sins, you are faithful and just to forgive my sins and cleanse me from all unrighteousness. Today, I confess that I have leaned on my understanding and put my trust in humans. I repent for every act of disobedience against your Word. Have mercy on me and cleanse me from all unrighteousness. I consecrate myself to you today. I renew my commitment to serve you and enter into a covenant to seek you. By the blood of the everlasting covenant, make me perfect in every good work and work in me that which is well-pleasing in your sight. I ask all these in Jesus' name. Thank you for your mercy. Thank you for your faithfulness. Thank you for the grace to live for you.

Prayer scriptures (1 John 1:9; Hebrews 13:20-21)

Intel/Prophetic Insights

DAY 20

She is like the merchants' ships; She bringeth her food from afar.

Proverbs 31:14 (KJV)

Merchant's ships are trading vessels, portals for transporting the goods of one kingdom to another. A Proverbs 31 warrior is a citizen of heaven (Philippians 3:20), and she understands that her work is to establish God's kingdom or dominion here on earth (Matthew 6:9-10). Hence, she consecrates herself as a vessel for various dimensions of God to find expression in the earthly realm.

We bring heaven's influence into the earth with the good news of the kingdom and prayer powered by the Holy Spirit. We transport the goods of the heavenly realm where God established his throne into the earth realm where the powers of darkness seek to dominate.

Consider these scriptures:

Matthew 6:9-10 (NKJV): *In this manner, therefore, pray: Our Father in heaven, Hallowed be Your name. Your kingdom come. Your will be done On earth as it is in heaven.*

Psalm 115:16 (NKJV): *The heaven, even the heavens, are the LORD's; But the earth He has given to the children of men.*

Matthew 28:18-20 (NKJV): *And Jesus came and spoke to them, saying, "All authority has been given to Me in heaven and on earth. Go therefore and make disciples of all the nations, baptizing them in the name of the Father and of the Son and of the Holy Spirit, teaching them to observe all things that I have commanded you; and lo, I am with you always, even to the end of the age." Amen.*

Declare this at least 100 times today: I AM GOD'S VESSEL. I TRANSPORT DIVINE GOODS FROM HEAVEN TO EARTH.

Intel/Prophetic Insights

DAY 21

She is like the merchants' ships; She bringeth her food from afar.

Proverbs 31:14 (KJV)

Food sustains us and keeps us alive. Food can also harm us depending on the source. Hence, a Proverbs 31 warrior, a citizen of heaven, brings her food from afar. God's Word is food from above, and God's Word makes us wise enough to refuse the poisonous foods the enemy tries to feed us (Psalm 119:98). As we study and meditate on God's Word, we increase in heavenly wisdom and bring the influence of heaven into the earth, establishing God's will in our family, finances, and every sphere of influence available to us.

Ponder this:

James 3:13-18 (NKJV): *Who is wise and understanding among you? Let him show by good conduct that his works are done in the meekness of wisdom. But if you have bitter envy and self-seeking in your hearts, do not boast and lie against the truth. This wisdom does not descend from above, but is earthly, sensual, demonic. For where envy and self-seeking exist, confusion and every evil thing are there.* **But the wisdom that is from**

above *is first pure, then peaceable, gentle, willing to yield, full of mercy and good fruits, without partiality and without hypocrisy. Now the fruit of righteousness is sown in peace by those who make peace.*

The world's standard for family life and other aspects of life will only dysregulate minds and bring destruction. God's standard for life brings peace to the home. When we operate with the wisdom from above, we will be present, full of mercy and empathy, and model truth in our households without hypocrisy.

Daily seek God for wisdom and pray for wisdom for members of your household (James 1:5; Luke 2:40; Proverbs 16:16; Job 28:18).

Intel/Prophetic Insights

Day 21

DAY 22

She riseth also while it is yet night, and giveth meat to her household, and a portion to her maidens.

Proverbs 31:15 (KJV)

Night is synonymous with darkness. The darkness he called night (Genesis 1:5) and 1 Thessalonians 5:5 (NKJV) says, "*You are all sons of light and sons of the day. We are not of the night nor of darkness.*" It takes light to eradicate darkness. The greater the darkness, the more intense the light required to subdue it. **In an intensely dark world, God's Word is light, the strong meat for our household and those under our leadership.**

Consider these scriptures:

Psalm 119:130 (NKJV): *The entrance of* **Your words gives light***; It gives understanding to the simple.*

Psalm 119:105 (NKJV): *Your word is* a lamp to my feet And **a light** to my path.

Proverbs 6:23 (AMP): *For **the commandment is a lamp, and the teaching [of the law] is light,** And reproofs (rebukes) for discipline are the way of life.*

Romans 13:11-13 (KJV): *And that, knowing the time, that now it is high time to awake out of sleep: for now is our salvation nearer than when we believed. The **night is far spent, the day is at hand: let us therefore cast off the works of darkness, and let us put on the armour of light.** Let us walk honestly, as in the day; not in rioting and drunkenness, not in chambering and wantonness, not in strife and envying.*

God's Word is Light, the Meat for Withstanding Darkness

The Word is light unto our path, bringing direction where confusion or uncertainty exists. When deciding which school to attend, which career choices to make, which sleepover invitations to accept, and so on, God's Word serves as an important light for our path. The light brings correction when darkness (rebellion, perversion, addiction, and other ungodly practices) tries to infiltrate our homes.

God's Word is Strong Meat

In the night, during moments of sorrow over our children and periods of weakness, let's remember that God's Word is meat for the spirit, soul, and body. God's Word nourishes the spirit, soul, and body (Proverbs 4:22). Speak God's Word in challenging times. Let's give God's Word as meat to our household when night terrors arise, peer pressure tries to derail our children, and the enemy tries to steal our peace, kill our dreams, and destroy the works of our hands.

Consider Hebrews 5:14 (KJV): *"strong meat belongeth to them that are of full age, even those who by reason of use have their senses exercised to discern both good and evil."* Feeding our household God's Word will help everyone discern good and evil in these last days and do the will of God. *Jesus saith unto them, My meat is to do the will of him that sent me, and to finish his work.* **John 4:34 (KJV).** Doing God's will becomes our household's meat, sustaining power, as we feed everyone God's meat through our actions and teaching the Word.

Intel/Prophetic Insights

DAY 23

She riseth also while it is yet night, and giveth meat to her household, and a portion to her maidens.

Proverbs 31:15 (KJV)

Teach Your Household God's Word

Hebrews 5:12-13 (KJV) says, *"For when for the time ye ought to be teachers, ye have need that one teach you again which be the first principles of the oracles of God; and are become such as have need of milk, and not of strong meat. For every one that useth milk is unskilful in the word of righteousness: for he is a babe."* We cannot give our household strong meat if we live on milk.

When we model living the Word and teach our household to do the same, we equip everyone in our household to enforce victory over the power of darkness and walk in authority.

Job 1:4-5 (NKJV) says, *And his sons would go and feast in their houses, each on his appointed day, and would send and invite their three sisters to eat and drink with them. So it was, when the days of feasting had run their course, that Job would send and sanctify them, and he would rise early in the morning and offer burnt offerings according to the number of them all. For Job said, "It may be that my sons have sinned and cursed God in their hearts." Thus Job did regularly.* Job's children became victims of spirit wars because they were not equipped to fight. Job was always sacrificing on their behalf, suggesting he didn't take the time to teach them to fight. Be intentional about inviting your spouse, children, and those in your sphere of influence to journey in the Word with you. Read, study, and meditate in the Word together.

Ensure that not a single day goes by without equipping yourself and your household with the Word. Have daily declarations. Proactively incubate truth in your spiritual womb through meditation.

As we read, study, and meditate on God's Word, we position ourselves to always walk in the light even in dark times (Proverbs 4:18; Psalm 119:105). When we expose ourselves to the light of the Word, growing in intimacy with God, we become a burning and shining light (John 5:35). When we repeatedly lean on God's Word in every season, we enhance our capacity to skillfully use God's Word to defeat whatever comes against us and those in our sphere of influence.

Prayer: Heavenly Father, thank you for the life-changing power of your Word. In the name of Jesus, open my spiritual eyes to understand your Word and destroy whatever hinders me from accessing divine revelation from your Word. Father, let your Word mix with faith in my heart and stir up the zeal for your Word. Thank you for answering my prayer! Alleluia!

Intel/Prophetic Insights

DAY 24

She considereth a field, and buyeth it: With the fruit of her hands she planteth a vineyard.

Proverbs 31:16 (KJV)

The field is synonymous with the world (Matthew 13:38; John 4:35). Matthew 13:38 (NKJV) says, *"The field is the world, the good seeds are the sons of the kingdom, but the tares are the sons of the wicked one."* A Proverbs 31 woman seeks to advance God's kingdom in and outside the home—souls must be won and discipled at home and outside the home. We must consider those playgrounds, our workplaces, grocery stores, mom groups, communities, cities, states, nations, and continents as field we need to buy, that is, take possession of for God's kingdom to be established. *Ask of Me, and I will give You The nations for Your inheritance, And the ends of the earth for Your possession.* **Psalm 2:8 (NKJV)**

The fruit turns the field (the world) into a vineyard where Jesus, the Vine is welcome (John 15:5). We bring the influence of Jesus into a place through the fruit of righteousness powered by the Holy Spirit. Proverbs 11:18 (NKJV) says, *"The wicked man does deceptive work,*

But he who sows righteousness will have a sure reward." The kingdom of heaven or the influence of Jesus is the vineyard we plant through righteousness. It involves laboring in prayer, evangelism, and other spiritual investments that lead people to Christ and establish them in the faith. We must be about our Father's business and guide our loved ones to sow into the spirit with us.

Declare these with all your heart at least 100 times today: I AM A FRUITFUL BRANCH. I MAKE SPIRITUAL INVESTMENTS.

Intel/Prophetic Insights

DAY 25

She considereth a field, and buyeth it: With the fruit of her hands she planteth a vineyard.

Proverbs 31:16 (KJV)

Consider the following scriptures:

Luke 9:61-62 (NKJV): *And another also said, "Lord, I will follow You, but let me first go and bid them farewell who are at my house." But Jesus said to him, "No one, having put his hand to the plow, and looking back, is fit for the kingdom of God.*

Colossians 4:12 (NKJV): *Epaphras, who is one of you, a bondservant of Christ, greets you, always laboring fervently for you in prayers, that you may stand perfect and complete in all the will of God.*

As we co-labor with God (1 Corinthians 3:6-9; 2 Corinthians 6:1; Mark 16:20) to turn many to righteousness and support their spiritual growth, the Spirit of wisdom begins to find expression through us, bringing heavenly solutions to earthly problems.

Those who are [spiritually] wise will shine brightly like the brightness of the expanse of heaven, and those who lead many to righteousness, [will shine] like the stars forever and ever. **Daniel 12:3 (AMP)**

The fruit of the [consistently] righteous is a tree of life, And he who is wise captures and wins souls [for God—he gathers them for eternity]. **Proverbs 11:30 (AMP)**

Have you considered a field you want to take for the kingdom of God? What strategies are you planning to implement to reach lost souls in your sphere of influence and beyond?

Consider these practices:

Use the map of the world or your nation's map to guide your family to pray for nations to become open to the gospel of Jesus Carry your children along when engaging in soul-winning outreaches.

Turn vacations into local and international mission trips.

Intel/Prophetic Insights

DAY 26

She girdeth her loins with strength, and strengtheneth her arms.

Proverbs 31:17 (KJV)

If you faint in the day of adversity, Your strength is small (Proverbs 24:10). For this reason, a Proverbs 31 warrior girds her loins and strengthens her arms. We live in challenging times requiring spiritual, mental, and physical strength to fulfill God's purpose for our lives and households. With unbiblical beliefs infiltrating the church and anti-Christ ideologies being imposed on us more than ever, we must be intentional about girding the loins to our minds, that is, proactively prepare our minds for action (1 Peter 1:13) so we can serve God wholeheartedly and not give in to deception. We must learn how to keep renewing our strength to finish our race.

Reflect: Assess your mind-girding endeavors. Are you addicted to the internet, social media, television, hanging out with friends who do not strengthen your spiritual growth, etc.? Are there relationships or activities that weaken you after making spiritual investments? How are you proactively expanding your mental and spiritual capacity to dispel false ideologies?

Intel/Prophetic Insights

Day 26

DAY 27

She girdeth her loins with strength, and strengtheneth her arms.

Proverbs 31:17 (KJV)

Girding your loins with strength for Priesthood and the Prophetic.

The loins are located between the upper and lower body, making them a seat of strength when using the body for various activities. The spiritual intelligence of a Proverbs 31 warrior is one reason she does not depend on her natural strength. She taps into a spiritual dimension for strength because natural strength has limits (1 Samuel 2:9). A cycle of defeat will continue until we acknowledge that the strength we need to overcome every adversity comes from God through His Spirit in us (Zechariah 4:6). We must accept the limits of human knowledge and expertise.

Several times in the Bible, God's priests and prophets received the instruction to gird their loins for service, to fulfil God's commandments (1 Kings 18:46; Jeremiah 1:17; Nahum 2:1). In addition, Psalm 93:1 (KJV) says, *"The LORD reigneth, he is clothed with majesty; the LORD is clothed with strength, wherewith he hath girded himself: the world also is stablished, that it cannot be moved."* With those scriptures in mind, we see that girding the loins with strength means a Proverbs 31 warrior does the following:

- She takes on the nature of Christ. Both Proverbs 31:17 and Proverbs 31:25 are revealed in the Lord's nature in Psalm 93:1.

- She strengthens her capacity to serve God as a priest and prophet (1 Peter 2:5 & 9; Jeremiah 1:5; Revelation 1:6), serving and leading those in her sphere of influence to advance God's kingdom. And serving God is a spiritual weapon (Jeremiah 51:20; Isaiah 41:15).

Intel/Prophetic Insights

DAY 28

> ***She girdeth her loins with strength***, *and strengtheneth her arms.*
>
> *Proverbs 31:17 (KJV)*

How can we strengthen our loins or the capacity to serve as priests and prophets?

- **Spiritual journeys in the Word:** Ephesians 6:14 tells us to gird our loins with truth and Jesus said, "Sanctify them by Your truth. Your word is truth." John 17:17 (NKJV)

- **Fasting:** Notable priests and prophets in the Bible--Moses, Daniel, Elijah, and our Lord, Jesus Christ engaged the power of fasting. Several times, Moses fasted 40 days and nights (Deut. 9:9-10; Exodus 24:18; Exodus 34:28) . Daniel fasted (Daniel 9:3; Daniel 10:2-3;). Elijah fasted (1 Kings 19:8). Jesus fasted, indicated that fasting should be a spiritual discipline, and shared that fasting is one of the secrets to greater dimensions of spiritual power (Matthew 4:2; Matthew 6:16-18; Matthew 17:14-21;). Fasting often is a sacrifice we must make to operate effectively in the prophetic. Are you willing to pay the price? We must master our natural appetite for food to maximize spiritual gifts and tap into spiritual frequencies required to access spiritual intel. We must fast proactively--we shouldn't fast only when unpleasant events occur. When we fast proactively for and with our family, emergency fasts will not be common in our households. We can teach our children to fast by carrying them along when we fast. Let's teach them why fasting is important. Consider starting your children off with one to three hours of fasting during weekends, and guide them to pray and focus on the Word when fasting.

- **Fervent and Consistent Pray Life:** Notable priests and prophets in the Bible--Moses, Daniel, Elijah, and our Lord, Jesus Christ were men of prayer. Moses was in constant communion with God. It was recorded that Daniel prayed three times a day (Daniel 6:10). Elijah's prayer life was highlighted in the New Testament (James 5:17). Jesus was a man of prayer--He prayed all night, and rose up early to pray (Luke 5:16; Luke 6:12; Luke 9:28; Mark 1:35; Matthew 14:23). Having a consistent prayer life is a sacrifice we must make. Are you willing to pay the price for priesthood and the prophetic? Praying all night, praying long hours, and rising up early to pray must become a lifestyle.

- **Fellowship with anointed people strengthens our priesthood and the prophetic (Psalm 84:7):** Transference of anointing. One of the wisest men that ever lived said, *"He who walks [as* *a companion] with wise men will be wise, But the companions of [conceited, dull-witted] fools [are fools themselves and] will experience harm."* Proverbs 13:20. (AMP) With wisdom and discernment, let's develop relationships with Christians who value and pursue spiritual gifts with utmost reverence for God's Word. Doing so will keep us grounded in the truth while modeling the power of godly association to our children.

Ponder this event: *After that you shall come to the hill of God where the Philistine garrison is. And it will happen, when you have come there to the city, that you will meet a group of prophets coming down from the high place with a stringed instrument, a tambourine, a flute, and a harp before them; and they will be prophesying. Then the Spirit of the Lord will come upon you, and you will prophesy with them and be turned into another man.* **1 Samuel 10:5-6 (NKJV)**

Assess the structures in place to ensure your priesthood is active and engaging the prophetic realm. Do you have daily dedicated times of prayer and word study? Do you have weekly fasting days? Who can hold you accountable to your commitments?

Intel/Prophetic Insights

DAY 29

She girdeth her loins with strength, and **strengtheneth her arms.**

Proverbs 31:17 (KJV)

The strengthening of her arms reminds me of Moses, a man once described as the meekest man on earth (Numbers 12:3). Exodus 17:12 (NIV) says, *"When Moses' hands grew tired, they took a stone and put it under him and he sat on it. Aaron and Hur held his hands up—one on one side, one on the other—so that his hands remained steady till sunset."* Despite all his encounters with God, Moses was humble enough to receive help from his brothers. He strengthened his leadership skills at one time by receiving wise counsel from his father-in-law (Exodus 18:13-26). God used other men to strengthen Moses' capacity to overcome challenges, and meekness positioned Moses to receive.

A Proverbs 31 warrior is not a lone ranger. Like Moses, she has battle buddies. A Proverbs 31 warrior maximizes divine relationships because she is meek. God gives grace to the humble, and grace for the strength to do God's will (1 Peter 5:5; Proverbs 3:34). Like Moses, a

Proverbs 31 warrior needs divine relationships for spiritual, mental, and physical strength. God wants us to be connected to other believers for fellowship and strength. That's why the Bible describes the Church, Zion, as the epicenter for receiving strength. Psalm 84:7 (KJV) says, *"They go from strength to strength, every one of them in Zion appeareth before God."* And Hebrews 12:22-23 (KJV) says, *" But you have come to Mount Zion and to the city of the living God, the heavenly Jerusalem, to an innumerable company of angels, to the general assembly and church of the firstborn who are registered in heaven, to God the Judge of all, to the spirits of just men made perfect".* In the New Testament, the Church is Zion. Oh, the depth of strength generated from fellowshipping in church with other believers!

I trivialized assembling with other believers until my eyes were opened to the difference between corporate and individual anointing. We need to experience God both in our homes and places of fellowship with other believers. That's one reason the scripture says, *"not forsaking our meeting together [as believers for worship and instruction], as is the habit of some, but encouraging one another; and all the more [faithfully] as you see the day [of Christ's return] approaching."* Hebrews 10:25 (AMP).

Psalm 92:13-14 (KJV) says, *"Those that be planted in the house of the LORD shall flourish in the courts of our God. They shall still bring forth fruit in old age; they shall be fat and flourishing."* To flourish means to thrive and develop in an extraordinary manner. That's what we need in our homes. We can't flourish without a strong church family. Let's get planted and nourished through fellowship with believers in places God has chosen to manifest his presence extravagantly. When parents are planted in the house of God, they point their children to a safe place to draw strength from in crisis.

Intel/Prophetic Insights

DAY 30

She girdeth her loins with strength, and **strengtheneth her arms.**

Proverbs 31:17 (KJV)

Fellowship and divine relationships are spiritual weapons. We need brothers and sisters whose prayers will set us free from life's prisons, in the days of persecution and trials of faith (Acts 12:5-11). We need divine relationships to stay strengthened in the faith. We need godly relationships to fully benefit from the spiritual gifts God has given to believers. I need you, and you need me. I have spiritual gifts you may not have, and you have unique gifts I do not possess—even if we have the same gifts, we may minister them differently based on our individual experiences. Developing relationships with fellow believers will strengthen us in good and bad times.

Be planted in a biblically grounded church. Ask God to lead you to the right church and align you with divine relationships.

Prayer: Heavenly Father, I thank you for the weapons of warfare you have made available to every believer and me. I acknowledge you are my source of strength. Today, I ask that you teach me to strengthen my loins and arms. By the power of your Spirit, help me to stand strong in the day of adversity. Open my spiritual eyes, ears, and mouth, and empower me to walk with you all the days of my life. I ask all these things in Jesus' name. Thank you for granting my request.

Assess your beliefs about the gathering of believers. How did you choose your church? How often do you attend church with your children? What changes can you implement to benefit from the power of fellowshipping with other believers?

Intel/Prophetic Insights

DAY 31

She perceiveth that her merchandise is good: her candle goeth not out by night.

Proverbs 31:18 (KJV)

To perceive reflects spiritual discernment, and the Holy Spirit gives us the capacity to discern. Merchandise is goods we can sell or buy. Consider the following scriptures:

Proverbs 23:23 (KJV) says, *Buy the truth, and sell it not; also wisdom, and instruction, and understanding.*

Revelation 3:18 (NKJV) says, *I counsel you to buy from Me gold refined in the fire, that you may be rich; and white garments, that you may be clothed, that the shame of your nakedness may not be revealed; and anoint your eyes with eye salve, that you may see.*

Isaiah 55:1 (NKJV) says, *Ho! Everyone who thirsts, Come to the waters; And you who have no money, Come, buy and eat. Yes, come, buy wine and milk Without money and without price.*

Matthew 13:44 (NKJV) says, *Again, the kingdom of heaven is like treasure hidden in a field, which a man found and hid; and for joy over it he goes and sells all that he has and buys that field.*

Using the aforementioned scriptures to interpret Proverbs 31:18, we can see that a Proverbs 31 woman invests in things of eternal value and protects what she values. If you are prioritizing your relationship with God or spiritual growth, you are buying truth, wisdom, instruction, and understanding and laying up eternal treasures for yourself. You must stay spiritually alert to keep the truth protected in your heart, make the most of your spiritual investments, and not get weary.

Leviticus 24:2 (NKJV) says, *Command the children of Israel that they bring to you pure oil of pressed olives for the light, to make the lamps burn continually.* As believers, we are now God's temple, where His Spirit dwells (1 Corinthians 3:16), and our lamps or candles (synonymous with our spirit) should burn continually in fellowship with the Holy Spirit.

Proverbs 20:27 tells us the spirit of a man is the candle of the Lord. A Proverbs 31 warrior's candle does not go out by night indicates spiritual alertness or sensitivity to the indwelling presence of the Holy Spirit. When our spirit is in communion with God's spirit, the night or darkness cannot put out our light. Intimacy with the Holy Spirit makes it more difficult to grieve and quench the Holy Spirit. Fellowship with the Holy Spirit is the core of spiritual intelligence—It heightens our understanding of God's Word, an essential key to accessing and effectively using all our spiritual weapons. Only a relationship with the Holy Spirit can keep us spiritually sensitive, empowering us to identify and effectively use spiritual weapons to navigate life triumphantly.

John 5:35 (AMP) says, *John was the lamp that kept on burning and shining [to show you the way], and you were willing for a while to rejoice in his light.* Like John, our lamps should be burning and shining to show those in our sphere of influence the Way, Jesus (John 14:6). We need the fire of God. We need to be baptized with the Holy Spirit and fire (Matthew 3:11). We need the spirit of fire that purifies, cleanses, and consecrates (Isaiah 4:4-5).

Meditate by declaring this at least 100 times today: I AM A BURNING AND SHINING LIGHT

Intel/Prophetic Insights

DAY 32

She perceiveth that her merchandise is good: her candle goeth not out by night.

Proverbs 31:18 (KJV)

The Holy Spirit is for you and your household

Then Peter said to them, Repent, and let every one of you be baptized in the name of Jesus Christ for the remission of sins; and you shall receive the gift of the Holy Spirit. For the promise is to you and to your children, and to all who are afar off, as many as the Lord our God will call. **Acts 2:38-39 (NKJV)**

One of the greatest ways to look well to our household's mental and spiritual wellness is to introduce everyone to the person of the Holy Spirit. As we develop a relationship with Him, let's ensure we carry members of our household, young and old, along.

Galatians 5:22-25 (KJV) says, *But the fruit of the Spirit is love, joy, peace, longsuffering, gentleness, goodness, faith, Meekness, temperance: against such there is no law. And they that are Christ's have crucified the flesh with the affections and lusts. If we live in the Spirit, let us also walk in the Spirit.* As we yield daily to the Holy Spirit, we begin to bear fruit that reveals His indwelling presence and our intimacy with Him. The fruit of the Spirit is produced when we crucify or master our fleshly desires—choosing the ways of the Spirit over natural desires.

1 Corinthians 14:1 (NKJV) says, *Pursue love, and desire spiritual gifts, but especially that you may prophesy.* And **1 Corinthians 12: 4-11 (NKJV)** says:

There are diversities of gifts, but the same Spirit. There are differences of ministries, but the same Lord. And there are diversities of activities, but it is the same God who works all in all. But the manifestation of the Spirit is given to each one for the profit of all: for to one is given the word of wisdom through the Spirit, to another the word of knowledge through the same Spirit, to another faith by the same Spirit, to another gifts of healings by the same Spirit, to another the working of miracles, to another prophecy, to another discerning of spirits, to another different kinds of tongues, to another the interpretation of tongues. But one and the same Spirit works all these things, distributing to each one individually as He wills.

As we partner with the Holy Spirit who knows all things, He will help us operate in these gifts when needed. We only need to possess the desire to have him help us and yield to His leading. We need these gifts for successful family life, career, business, ministry, etc. When we produce outstanding results with the help of the Holy Spirit, we reveal Jesus Christ to the world and bring people to the light.

To receive the baptism of the Holy Spirit, pray this:

Heavenly Father, thank you for the gift of the Holy Spirit. Your Word says you will give the Holy Spirit to those who ask you. I ask for your Holy Spirit to dwell in me and come upon me this moment in the name of Jesus.

Assess your household's awareness of the Holy Spirit and your relationship with Him. Are members of your household filled with the Holy Spirit? Do you speak with the Holy Spirit daily? Are you utilizing your spiritual gifts?

Intel/Prophetic Insights

Day 32

DAY 33

She layeth her hands to the spindle, And her hands hold the distaff.

Proverbs 31:19 (KJV)

The Orthodox Jewish Bible says, She layeth her *Yadayim* to the distaff, and her fingers lay hold of the spindle. (Mishle 31:19 TOJB2011). *Yadayim* means hands. Considering the Proverbs 31 woman's identity as a woman of valor, the words of David, the warrior, come to mind. **Psalm 144:1** (KJV) declares, *A Psalm of David. Blessed be the LORD my strength, which teacheth my hands to war, and my fingers to fight.* As a soldier of Christ (2 Timothy 2:3-4; Ephesians 6:11), a Proverbs 31 woman is called to a life of spiritual warfare, fighting the good fight of faith and contending for the faith.

1 Timothy 6:12 (KJV) says, *Fight the good fight of faith, lay hold on eternal life, whereunto thou art also called, and hast professed a good profession before many witnesses.* **Jude 1:3** (KJV) says, *Beloved, when I gave all diligence to write unto you of the common salvation, it was needful for me to write unto you, and exhort you that ye should earnestly contend for the faith which was once delivered unto the saints.*

The dictionary definition of a distaff sheds a little light on how a Proverbs 31 warrior divides the Word of truth and serves in God's kingdom, earnestly contending for the faith. The Britannica dictionary describes a distaff as a device used in hand spinning in which individual fibres are drawn out of a mass of prepared fibres held on a stick (the distaff), twisted together to form a continuous strand, and wound on a second stick (the spindle). It is most often used for making linen.

2 Timothy 2:15 (AMP) says, *Study and do your best to present yourself to God approved, a workman [tested by trial] who has no reason to be ashamed, accurately handling and skillfully teaching the word of truth.* I picture a Proverbs 31 warrior studying God's Word and accurately handling and skillfully teaching the word of truth like the handling of a distaff and spindle. That's warfare! That's how we contend for the faith, ensuring God's Word is not blasphemed nor rendered ineffective.

Titus 2:3-5 (KJV) says: *The aged women likewise, that they be in behaviour as becometh holiness, not false accusers, not given to much wine, teachers of good things; That they may teach the young women to be sober, to love their husbands, to love their children, To be discreet, chaste, keepers at home, good, obedient to their own husbands, that the word of God be not blasphemed.* A Proverbs 31 warrior lives the Word. She also recognizes and performs the duty of supporting the spiritual growth of other women, dispelling doubts about the transforming and living power of the gospel.

A proverbs 31 warrior is a kingdom builder, a workman in God's kingdom. She rightly divides the Word of truth so she and those around her are living righteously and the Word of God is not blasphemed.

Intel/Prophetic Insights

DAY 34

She layeth her hands to the spindle, And her hands hold the distaff.

Proverbs 31:19 (KJV)

Exodus 35:24-26 (NKJV) says: *Everyone who offered an offering of silver or bronze brought the Lord's offering. And everyone with whom was found acacia wood for any work of the service, brought it. All the women who were gifted artisans spun yarn with their hands, and brought what they had spun, of blue, purple, and scarlet, and fine linen. And all the women whose hearts stirred with wisdom spun yarn of goats' hair.* The products derived from hand spinning with the distaff and spindle were used for beautifying the temple and clothing the priests. A Proverbs 31 warrior serves in God's house. She is a responsible church member who is intentional about serving God's people, fellow priests in the royal priesthood.

Ephesians 4:11-14 (KJV) says, *And He Himself gave some to be apostles, some prophets, some evangelists, and some pastors and teachers, for the equipping of the saints for the work of ministry, for the edifying of the body of Christ, till we all come to the unity of the faith and of the* *knowledge of the Son of God, to a perfect man, to the measure of the stature of the fullness of Christ; that we should no longer be children, tossed to and fro and carried about with every wind of doctrine, by the trickery of men, in the cunning craftiness of deceitful plotting.*

As a member of the royal priesthood and body of Christ, a Proverbs 31 warrior is equipped for service and participates in the equipping of the saints for the work of ministry.

A Proverbs 31 woman spiritually beautifies the body of Christ through her financial resources, raising godly children, ministering to other women, and equipping the saints.

As we serve God's people, we actively participate in creating a space where our families can receive spiritual, social, and emotional support. *For God is not unjust to forget your work and labor of love which you have shown toward His name, in that you have ministered to the saints, and do minister.* **Hebrews 6:10 (NKJV)**

Assess your discipleship skills and church involvement. Are you serving, and why are you serving in the church? How are you supporting the spiritual growth of women in your sphere of influence?

Intel/Prophetic Insights

DAY 35

She stretcheth out her hand to the poor; yea, she reacheth forth her hands to the needy.

Proverbs 31:20 (KJV)

Giving expands the capacity for mindsight, empathy and self-awareness. When you and your household give to the poor and needy with your spiritual values in mind, you experience the following:

- You become more selfless
- You easily empathize with the challenges others face
- You bear other people's burden without self-promotion
- You see yourselves as an agent of change
- You reduce the risks for depression

A Proverbs 31 warrior is endued with the giving grace; hence, she is constantly seeking opportunities to bless the poor and needy. **2 Corinthians 8:7 (NIV)** says, *But since you excel in everything—in faith, in speech, in knowledge, in complete earnestness and in the love we have kindled in you* —***see that you also excel in this grace of giving.***

Grace is the empowerment to do what is humanly impossible, and grace multiplies as we grow in the knowledge of the Father and Son (2 Peter 1:2). When we become intimate with God the Father and God the Son, we take on the nature of giving. God gave His best, Jesus. Jesus gave His life and modeled selflessness. Those who KNOW Elohim are supernatural givers.

Stretching forth and reaching forth her hands indicates cheerfully seeking opportunities to give or bless others, picking people up from their place of lack, and being a conduit of provision for the poor and needy. Giving to those who cannot give back to us is proof of love and a reflection of the state of our hearts. *But whoever has this world's goods, and sees his brother in need, and shuts up his heart from him, how does the love of God abide in him?* **1 John 3:17 (NKJV)**

When we adopt giving as a kingdom lifestyle and allow our household to participate in the act of giving, we model and foster a culture of selflessness. More importantly, we teach our household that it is more blessed to give to others and God rewards those who give to the poor.

Ponder these scriptures:

I have shown you in every way, by laboring like this, that you must support the weak. And remember the words of the Lord Jesus, that He said, 'It is more blessed to give than to receive.' **Acts 20:35 (NKJV)**

He who has pity on the poor lends to the LORD, And He will pay back what he has given. **Proverbs 19:17 (NKJV)**

Whoever shuts his ears to the cry of the poor Will also cry himself and not be heard. **Proverbs 21:13 (NKJV)**

He who gives to the poor will not lack, But he who hides his eyes will have many curses. **Proverbs 28:27 (NKJV)**

He who oppresses the poor taunts and insults his Maker, But he who is kind and merciful and gracious to the needy honors Him. **Proverbs 14:31 (AMP)**

For thou hast been a strength to the poor, a strength to the needy in his distress, a refuge from the storm, a shadow from the heat, when the blast of the terrible ones is as a storm against the wall. **Isaiah 25:4 (KJV)**

Assess your giving lifestyle. Do you give cheerfully and bountifully? Do you guide your children to give? Do you seek opportunities to help others? Are you preoccupied with the thought that people will abuse your generosity? Do you give for recognition and expect reward from those you help?

Prayer: Heavenly Father, thank you for your Word concerning giving. In the name of Jesus, endue me with the giving grace and free my heart from coveteousness.

Intel/Prophetic Insights

Day 35

DAY 36

She is not afraid of the snow for her household: for all her household are clothed with scarlet.

Proverbs 31:21 (KJV)

The scarlet represents the blood of Jesus. Snow symbolizes the harsh realities and seasons of life. Our families will face trials, and we will experience ministry or career challenges, but we can ALWAYS emerge victorious. By the blood of Jesus, we can navigate difficult seasons fearlessly.

Revelation 12:11 (AMP) declares, *And they overcame and conquered him because of the blood of the Lamb and because of the word of their testimony, for they did not love their life and renounce their faith even when faced with death.* The blood of Jesus has secured victory for us. We fight from a position of victory when we live conscious of this truth and plead the blood of Jesus as a defense against the enemy's attacks. More than ever, we must engage the power in the blood of Jesus and seek a deeper revelation of the power in the blood of Jesus.

Understanding the power in the blood of Jesus will shift how you exercise your spiritual authority. Take a moment to pray this with all your heart before studying and meditating on the subsequent scriptures.

Pray: Father, I thank you for your Word and Spirit. I receive the Spirit of wisdom and revelation. Let the eyes of my understanding be enlightened in the name of Jesus.

Study the following scriptures:

We apply the Blood of Jesus for *Divine Protection and Memorial of the Finished Works of Jesus, Our Passover Lamb*

For the Lord will pass through to strike the Egyptians; and when He sees the blood on the lintel and on the two doorposts, the Lord will pass over the door and not allow the destroyer to come into your houses to strike you. And you shall observe this thing as an ordinance for you and your sons forever. It will come to pass when you come to the land which the Lord will give you, just as He promised, that you shall keep this service. And it shall be, when your children say to you, 'What do you mean by this service?' that you shall say, 'It is the Passover sacrifice of the Lord, who passed over the houses of the children of Israel in Egypt when He struck the Egyptians and delivered our households.' **Exodus 12:23-27 (NKJV)**

Knowing that you were not redeemed with corruptible things, like silver or gold, from your aimless conduct received by tradition from your fathers, but with the precious blood of Christ, as of a lamb without blemish and without spot. **1 Peter 1:18-19 (NKJV)**

For I received from the Lord that which I also delivered to you: that the Lord Jesus on the same night in which He was betrayed took bread; and when He had given thanks, He broke it and said, "Take, eat; this is My body which is broken for you; do this in remembrance of Me." In the same manner He also took the cup after supper, saying, "This cup is the new covenant in My blood. This do, as often as you drink it, in remembrance of Me." For as often as you eat this bread and drink this cup, you proclaim the Lord's death till He comes. **1 Corinthians 11:23-26 (NKJV)**

Intel/Prophetic Insights

DAY 37

She is not afraid of the snow for her household: for all her household are clothed with scarlet.

Proverbs 31:21 (KJV)

Pray: Father, I thank you for your Word and Spirit. I receive the Spirit of wisdom and revelation. Let the eyes of my understanding be enlightened in the name of Jesus.

Apply the Blood of Jesus for Continuous Cleansing

For if the blood of bulls and goats and the ashes of a heifer, sprinkling the unclean, sanctifies for the purifying of the flesh, how much more shall **the blood of Christ, who through the eternal Spirit offered Himself without spot to God, cleanse your conscience from dead works** *to serve the living God?* **Hebrews 9:13-14 (NKJV)**

Now may the God of peace who brought up our Lord Jesus from the dead, that great Shepherd of the sheep, **through the blood of the everlasting covenant, make you complete** *in every good work to do His will, working in you what is well pleasing in His sight, through Jesus Christ, to whom be glory forever and ever. Amen.* **Hebrews 13:20-21 (NKJV)**

Assess your beliefs about the Holy Communion and the appropriation of Jesus' blood. Why do you or do you not partake in the Holy Communion? How often and when do you appropriate or apply the blood of Jesus?

Intel/Prophetic Insights

DAY 38

She is not afraid of the snow for her household: for all her household are clothed with scarlet.

Proverbs 31:21 (KJV)

Consider practicing the following:

- Take the communion with your family. Make it a moment of reflection and consider asking what each member desires from the Lord's table
- Put the blood of Jesus on your family and property
- Always ask God to cleanse members of your household
- Pray Hebrews 13:20-21 often

Prayer: Father, I thank you for making me a virtuous woman. I thank you for the blood of Jesus. I draw the bloodline for defense against every attack on my household. By the blood of Jesus, I decree the deliverance of my household from all forces against our spiritual growth. By the blood of Jesus, I destroy all interferences of the enemy against the fulfillment of God's purpose for our lives. Thank you, Father, for victory! Alleluia!

Intel/Prophetic Insights

DAY 39

She maketh herself coverings of tapestry; her clothing is silk and purple.

Proverbs 31:22 (KJV)

Consecration for Priesthood

A Proverbs 31 warrior's coverings and clothing are made from materials used for priestly garments required for consecrated service in the courts of God. In the Old Testament, priestly garments were not made by ordinary men without a heart for God, and God anointed people with skills for this assignment. **Exodus 35:34-35 (NKJV)** says: *And He has put in his heart the ability to teach, in him and Aholiab the son of Ahisamach, of the tribe of Dan. He has filled them with skill to do all manner of work of the engraver and the designer and the tapestry maker, in blue, purple, and scarlet thread, and fine linen, and of the weaver—those who do every work and those who design artistic works.*

God may not have favorites, but He has intimates, individuals who have chosen a life of consecration to Him. A Proverbs 31 warrior chooses a life of consecration to God, yielding herself as an instrument of worship to God. She is sacrificially available when summoned to pray for the needs of others, give, fast, etc. She gives up fleshly desires to keep herself clothed and covered, preserving her consecration for service.

1 Peter 2:9-12 (AMP) says: *But you are A CHOSEN RACE, A royal PRIESTHOOD, A CONSECRATED NATION, A [special] PEOPLE FOR God's OWN POSSESSION, so that you may proclaim the excellencies [the wonderful deeds and virtues and perfections] of Him who called you out of darkness into His marvelous light. Once you were NOT A PEOPLE [at all], but now you are GOD'S PEOPLE; once you had NOT RECEIVED MERCY, but now you have RECEIVED MERCY.*

Beloved, I urge you as aliens and strangers [in this world] to abstain from the sensual urges [those dishonorable desires] that wage war against the soul. Keep your behavior excellent among the [unsaved] Gentiles [conduct yourself honorably, with graciousness and integrity], so that for whatever reason they may slander you as evildoers, yet by observing your good deeds they may [instead come to] glorify God in the day of visitation [when He looks upon them with mercy.

We have been chosen for priesthood to stand in the gap, reconcile people to God, and break generational curses on behalf of our families. Like Abraham, Noah, and Rahab, our priesthood can save our families. Like Jesus, our priesthood can save many souls. *Seeing then that we have a great High Priest who has passed through the heavens, Jesus the Son of God, let us hold fast our confession. For we do not have a High Priest who cannot sympathize with our weaknesses, but was in all points tempted as we are, yet without sin. Let us therefore come boldly to the throne of grace, that we may obtain mercy and find grace to help in time of need.* **Hebrews 4:14-16 (NKJV)**

Assess your understanding of your priestly role in your home and the body of Christ. Why do you pray and What do you pray for? Why do you fast? What does a consecrated life mean to you? Ask God to show you your consecrations.

Intel/Prophetic Insights

DAY 40

She maketh fine linen, and selleth it; and delivereth girdles unto the merchant.

Proverbs 31:24 (KJV)

Fine linen is a material for clothing and beautifying priests, and selling indicates a spiritual transaction. For example, we can buy truth (Proverbs 23:23) with hunger and humility, which are spiritual currencies a believer must possess for spiritual growth. Also consider **Revelation 3:18 (KJV):** *I counsel thee to buy of me gold tried in the fire, that thou mayest be rich; and white raiment, that thou mayest be clothed, and that the shame of thy nakedness do not appear; and anoint thine eyes with eyesalve, that thou mayest see.* Buying and selling in God's kingdom is a call to engage in spiritual transactions with currencies such as sacrifice, humility, faith, etc.

Like the Proverbs 31 warrior, the merchants are royal priests and fellow kingdom citizens of heaven establishing God's will in the earth with heavenly resources (wisdom, righteousness, justice, etc.). Through spiritual transactions, a Proverbs 31 warrior strengthens others in the body of Christ.

Selling fine linen and delivering girdles means a Proverbs 31 warrior brings out the best and strengthens fellow believers or those in the royal priesthood. To deepen our understanding of the role a Proverbs 31 warrior plays in strengthening or edifying those in the body of Christ, ponder the following scriptures highlighting the importance of girdles in priesthood:

*And for Aaron's sons thou shalt make coats, and thou shalt **make for them girdles**, and bonnets shalt thou make for them, **for glory and for beauty**.* **Exodus 28:40 (KJV)**

*And thou shalt speak unto all that are wise hearted, whom I have filled with the spirit of wisdom, that they may **make Aaron's garments to consecrate him, that he may minister unto me in the priest's office**. And these are the garments which they shall make; a breastplate, and an ephod, and a robe, and a broidered coat, a mitre, and a girdle: and they shall **make holy garments for Aaron thy brother, and his sons, that he may minister unto me in the priest's office**. And they shall take gold, and blue, and purple, and scarlet, and **fine linen**.* **Exodus 28:3-5 (KJV)**

*And to her was granted that she should be arrayed in fine linen, clean and white: **for the fine linen is the righteousness of saints**.* **Revelation 19:8 (KJV)**

*And I will clothe him with thy robe, and **strengthen him with thy girdle**, and I will commit thy government into his hand: and he shall be* *a father to the inhabitants of Jerusalem, and to the house of Judah.* **Isaiah 22:21 (KJV)**

A Proverbs 31 woman cannot be found causing strife or gossiping about fellow believers. She is secure in her relationship with God, understands her unique assignment, and ministers righteousness. Moments with a Proverbs 31 warrior are edifying, stirring hunger for God and love for God's people. With this type of lifestyle, a Proverbs 31 Warrior's children will have a positive perception of those in the body of Christ and consider the Church a safe space.

Intel/Prophetic Insights

DAY 41

Strength and honour are her clothing; and she shall rejoice in time to come.

Proverbs 31:25 (KJV)

Strength and honor are her clothing, and she can laugh at the days to come.

Proverbs 31:25 (BSB)

God wants you full of joy, and I want you to believe it.

I love the BSB and KJV translations of Proverbs 31:25 because the declarations that "she shall rejoice" and "she can laugh at" offer hope for the future and call us to respond to life's events with an awareness of our identity. Perhaps you have not laughed in a while or don't believe it is possible to rejoice even in challenging times; I pray that completing this section will stir up joy and birth a mental shift that will cause you to rejoice in every season of life.

To renew your mind and clear up all doubts that the joyful life described in Proverbs 31:25 is God's desire for you, I invite you to meditate on these scriptures:

Always be joyful. **1 Thessalonians 5:16 (NLT)**

Always be full of joy in the Lord. I say it again—rejoice! **Philippians 4:4 (NLT)**

For the Kingdom of God is not a matter of what we eat or drink, but of living a life of goodness, peace, and joy in the Holy Spirit. **Romans 14:17 (NLT)**

But let all who take refuge in you rejoice; let them sing joyful praises forever. Spread your protection over them, that all who love your name may be filled with joy. **Psalm 5:11 (NLT)**

Since God wants you full of joy so you can laugh at the days to come, you can lean on Him as the source of your joy in good and challenging times. You are an overcomer living in a fallen world filled with trials and challenges that can only bring out the best in you. Believe the Words of Jesus, *What is impossible for people is possible with God.* **Luke 18:27 (NLT)**

Intel/Prophetic Insights

Day 41

DAY 42

Strength and honour are her clothing; and she shall rejoice in time to come.

Proverbs 31:25 (KJV)

How can we make strength and honor our clothing so we can laugh at the days to come? **By Putting on Christ.** Our Lord, Jesus Christ, is our strength and honor clothing—He has won every battle for us and equipped us with the full armor required to enforce victory. That's why the Bible says, *When troubles of any kind come your way, consider it an opportunity for great joy.* **James 1:2 (NLT)**

Consider these scriptures:

"The LORD reigneth, he is clothed with majesty; **the LORD is clothed with strength**, wherewith he hath girded himself: the world also is established, that it cannot be moved." **Psalm 93:1 (KJV)**

"Bless the LORD, O my soul. **O LORD my God, thou art very great; thou art clothed with honour** and majesty." **Psalm 104:1 (KJV)**

With those scriptures in mind, we are not solely responsible for clothing ourselves with strength and honor. Since the Lord is clothed with honor and strength, when we put on Christ through salvation and daily accept His Lordship over our lives, we take on Christ's nature-- clothed with honor and strength.

Putting on Christ through salvation:

Galatians 3:26-27 (NKJV) says, *For you are all sons of God through faith in Christ Jesus. For as many of you as were baptized into Christ have put on Christ.*

Salvation brings us into God's realm. Therefore, amid earthly adversities, we can laugh at days to come because we are spirit beings highly ranked in the heavenly realms, seated in Christ Jesus far above all principality and powers. **Ephesians 2:4-6 (KJV)** says, *But God, who is rich in mercy, because of His great love with which He loved us, even when we were dead in trespasses, made us alive together with Christ (by grace you have been saved), and raised us up together, and made us sit together in the heavenly places in Christ Jesus.*

Psalm 2:1-4 (KJV) declares, *Why do the heathen rage, And the people imagine a vain thing? The kings of the earth set themselves, and the rulers take counsel together, Against the LORD, and against his anointed, saying, Let us break their bands asunder, And cast away their cords from us. He that sitteth in the heavens shall laugh: The Lord shall have them in derision.*

Our Lord is not worried about the future and demonic agendas. And His desire is for everyone under His Lordship to live fearlessly and anxious for nothing. We must live conscious of whose and who we are—We are the redeemed of the Lord, fighting from a position of victory to reveal the manifold wisdom of God in heaven and earth realms. Despite the trials we face and the intense darkness in the world, we can rejoice always and laugh at the days to come because He who sits in heaven laughs. As he is, so are we in this world (1 John 4:17).

Intel/Prophetic Insights

DAY 43

Strength and honour are her clothing; and she shall rejoice in time to come.

Proverbs 31:25 (KJV)

Putting on Christ by accepting His Lordship

How can we make strength and honor our clothing so we can laugh at the days to come? By Putting on Christ. Today, we will explore putting on Christ by accepting His Lordship—living a life surrendered to Christ with a burning desire to see His will established in our sphere of influence. **Romans 13:13-14 (KJV)** says, *Let us walk properly, as in the day, not in revelry and drunkenness, not in lewdness and lust, not in strife and envy. But put on the Lord Jesus Christ, and make no provision for the flesh, to fulfill its lusts.* When we accept Jesus Christ as our Lord, we yield to Him daily, crucifying the flesh through the help of the Holy Spirit. The proof of true repentance and gratitude for our salvation is to submit ourselves daily to God, seeking to please Him in all we do. When we live to please the one who delivered us from the power of darkness, the prince of this world will have nothing in us, and there will be no opening for the thief to legally steal, kill, and destroy. Give no opportunity to the devil; do not give the devil a foothold or place (Ephesians 4:27).

When tempted to engage in immorality, gossip, abore bitterness, live in unforgiveness, etc., let's remember that the enemy constantly seeks opportunities to steal our joy. We must guard joy as our birthright in Christ.

Psalm 35:27 declares, *Let those who delight in my righteousness shout for joy and be glad and say evermore, "Great is the LORD, who delights in the welfare of his servant!"* Psalm 35:27 is a prophetic declaration that our delight in righteousness, seeking and adopting God's way of doing life, is guaranteed to keep us in the realm of joy.

Seeking God's way of doing life will drive you to feed on God's Word daily, strengthening your faith in God's faithfulness to take care of all that concerns you and your household. Adopting God's way of life will empower you to walk in the light, run away from sin, put devils in their place of defeat, and live fearlessly.

Take the pressure off yourself and lean on the Holy Spirit to help you crucify the flesh daily, making no provision for the desires of the flesh to master you. **Philippians 2:13 (AMP)** declares, *For it is [not your strength, but it is] God who is effectively at work in you, both to will and to work [that is, strengthening, energizing, and creating in you the longing and the ability to fulfill your purpose] for His good pleasure."*

I pray that the God of peace who brought up our Lord Jesus from the dead, that great Shepherd of the sheep, through the blood of the everlasting covenant, make you complete in every good work to do His will, working in you what is well pleasing in His sight, through Jesus Christ, to whom be glory forever and ever. Amen. **Hebrews 13:20-21 (NKJV)**

Take a moment to reflect on God's goodness and laugh.

Intel/Prophetic Insights

DAY 44

She openeth her mouth with wisdom; and in her tongue is the law of kindness.

Proverbs 31:26 (KJV)

The tongue is a powerful tool for regulating ourselves and family members. James 3:6-12 (NKJV) says: *And the tongue is a fire, a world of iniquity. The tongue is so set among our members that it defiles the whole body, and sets on fire the course of]nature; and it is set on fire by hell. For every kind of beast and bird, of reptile and creature of the sea, is tamed and has been tamed by mankind. But no man can tame the tongue. It is an unruly evil, full of deadly poison. With it we bless our God and Father, and with it we curse men, who have been made in the similitude of God. Out of the same mouth proceed blessing and cursing. My brethren, these things ought not to be so.*

The natural man cannot tame the tongue. It takes supernatural power to tame the tongue. A Proverbs 31 warrior masters her tongue and regulates her family space with words and divine wisdom through the following practices:

Meditation: *This Book of the Law shall not depart from your mouth, but you shall meditate in it day and night, that you may observe to do according to all that is written in it. For then you will make your way prosperous, and then you will have good success.* **Joshua 1:8 (NKJV)** Spirit, soul, and body prosperity, and good success in life are made possible by consistently speaking and pondering the Word.

Out of the abundance of the heart, the mouth speaks (Luke 6:45). Therefore, we must consistently eat the Word, and allow the Word to dwell richly in us (Colossians 3:16) if we want to speak life (John 6:63), bringing God-class success into the earth realm. Like David, this should be our prayer, *Let the words of my mouth and the meditation of my heart Be acceptable in Your sight, O LORD, my strength and my Redeemer.* **Psalm 19:14 (NKJV)**

Yielding the tongue to the Holy Spirit: Intimacy with the Holy Spirit empowers us to dominate the flesh, manifesting the divine nature of kindness. But the Holy Spirit produces this kind of fruit in our lives: love, joy, peace, patience, **kindness**, goodness, faithfulness (Galatians 5:22).

Mark 16:17 (NKJV) says, *And these signs will follow those who believe. In My name they will cast out demons; they will speak with **new tongues**.* The Holy Spirit renews our tongue, giving us the capacity to speak in tongues (gift) and master our tongue (fruit). Building up yourself in the most Holy faith, praying in the Holy Ghost. Jude 1:20

Psalm 34:12-13 (KJV) says, *Who is the man who desires life, And loves many days, that he may see good? Keep your tongue from evil, And your lips from speaking deceit.* A Proverbs 31 woman embraces the benefits of speaking life; hence, she is intentional about mastering her mouth and emotions, enabling her to speak life.

Practice: Speak life daily and guide members of your household to do the same. Go beyond daily affirmations. Step into the prophetic by speaking spirit and life. Declare scriptures over your life and family. Write at least 5 scriptures you will begin to declare over your household daily.

Intel/Prophetic Insights

DAY 45

> *She openeth her mouth with wisdom; and in her tongue is the law of kindness.*
>
> *Proverbs 31:26 (KJV)*

Negative words are predominantly spoken during moments of anger. Anger is both an emotion and a spirit. Anger is an emotion that can be influenced or exploited by spirits. It is okay to feel angry or frustrated, but allowing these emotions to rule us is not okay. God wants us to master our feelings or emotions. We must bring our thoughts and emotions under the control of our spirit in communion with the Holy Spirit (1 Corinthians 9:27). *"Be angry, and do not sin": do not let the sun go down on your wrath.* **Ephesians 4:26 (NKJV)** *Understand this, my beloved brothers and sisters. Let everyone be quick to hear [be a careful, thoughtful listener], slow to speak [a speaker of carefully chosen words and], slow to anger [patient, reflective, forgiving].* James 1:19 (AMP) In moments of frustration and anger, we can speak mindfully by using the STOP strategy:

Stop. Be slow to respond. Give yourself a moment to take charge of the situation. Take a deep breath. Control your breathing. It is one way to tell your body you control it.

Take a deep breath. Control your breathing. It is one way to tell your body you control it.

Observe your emotional and spiritual state and those you are interacting with. This is the time to rebuke the spirit of fear and anger in the name of Jesus—bring them under your control. This is the time to reject the negative emotional signal you may be receiving from another by giving others the benefit of the doubt.

Plan your response before responding. Silence is a response. We can only respond out of the abundance of our hearts. We cannot be full of love and respond with hate. Hence, we must purposefully choose what we give our thoughts and attention to (Philippians 4:8). This is one reason we must consistently meditate on God's Word and pray.

These spiritual practices empower us to respond with God's love in difficult situations. When loved ones betray us, people persecute us, and we are treated unjustly, the abundance of God's truth in our hearts makes it easier to forgive and respond with love. *Keep actively watching and praying that you may not come into temptation; the spirit is willing, but the body is weak.* **Matthew 26:41 (AMP)**

Prayer: Heavenly Father, thank You for being mindful of me. I ask for the grace to live a life that is pleasing to You. Teach me to be mindful of You and others, and empower me to master my emotions. In Jesus' name.

Declare this at least 100 times today: I OPEN MY MOUTH WITH WISDOM. IN MY TONGUE IS THE LAW OF KINDNESS.

Intel/Prophetic Insights

DAY 46

She looks well to the ways of her household, And does not eat the bread of idleness.

Proverbs 31:27 (KJV)

Looking well involves being spiritually, mentally, and physically present to meet the needs of our households. Eating the bread of idleness connotes experiencing the consequences of laziness and slothfulness. A Proverbs 31 warrior is not careless or ignorant. She works for the family life she desires, foresees danger, and labors to ensure her household is holistically well.

Ecclesiastes 10:18 (NKJV) says, *Because of laziness the building decays, And through idleness of hands the house leaks.* Spiritual laziness, an unwillingness to engage in the spiritual disciplines necessary for expanding spiritual sensitivity and exercising spiritual authority is costly. Ungodly ideologies, activities of demonic altars in our communities, and all manner of dysfunctions will infiltrate or leak into our homes if we do not take charge of our household's activities. A Proverbs 31 warrior exerts territorial authority in her home (alongside a present spouse). She takes charge of the physical nourishment of the household to avoid preventable diseases, support healthy development, and ensure the physical bodies in her home are preserved long enough to host God's spirit. A Proverbs 31 warrior looks well to the mental wellness of her household by enhancing emotional intelligence in the home, supporting her family member's capacity for self-regulation, self-awareness, empathy, social skills, and so on. She creates a nurturing and responsive environment and acquires strategic knowledge for the general well-being of her household (including herself).

Prayer: Heavenly Father, I thank you for my household. By your Spirit, teach me how to look well to the ways of my household and strengthen me to do what it takes to be a woman of valor. Father, open my eyes to see all I need to correct and specific resources for my family's wellbeing. I ask all these in Jesus' name. Thank you, Father!

Reflect: How are you looking well to screentime management in your home? How are you guarding your children's minds from negative influences? How often do you proactively engage with parenting and marriage books, videos, or courses? What relationships or activities do you need to terminate? What are your family values and boundaries?

Intel/Prophetic Insights

DAY 47

Her children arise and call her blessed; her husband also, and he praises her

Proverbs 31:28 (NIV)

Receiving honor from members of one's household is uncommon (Mark 6:4-5). A Proverbs 31 warrior receives an uncommon reward, praise from her closest family members.

The Holy Spirit is the greatest blessing available to a Proverbs 31 warrior. The Holy Spirit empowers us to love our children with the God kind of love (1 Corinthians 13:4-8). The Holy Spirit gives us the discernment we need to guide our children in the right direction (1 Corinthians 12:10). The Holy Spirit empowers us to heal our children's physical and inner wounds (1 Corinthians 12:9). The Holy Spirit helps us intercede when we can't make sense of motherhood (Romans 8:36-37).

The spiritual investments and sacrifices we make for our children are the greatest blessings we can give them. And being a blessing compels people to call us blessed. Doing family life powered by the Holy Spirit is the reason our children will ARISE and CALL us BLESSED, and our spouses will PRAISE US. The praise or recognition we desire from our spouses and children depends on our intimacy with the Holy Spirit. We earn honor; we don't demand it. **Proverbs 31:30 (NKJV)** says, *But a woman who fears the Lord, she shall be praised.* When we yield to the Spirit of the fear of the Lord, our decisions and lifestyle will ultimately earn us praise.

Imagine and declare this truth at least 100 times today: MY CHILDREN ARISE AND CALL ME BLESSED; MY HUSBAND ALSO, AND HE PRAISES ME.

Intel / Prophetic Insights

DAY 48

Many daughters have done well, But you excel them all.

Proverbs 31:29 (NKJV)

A Proverbs 31 warrior excels because her identity is in Christ, she pursues her unique assignment in Christ, and those who know their God shall be strong and do exploit (Daniel 11:32). When we have a relationship with God, we gain access to supernatural intel that sets us apart - We do well beyond natural capacities. We excel with consistency and diligence in growing our relationship with God. As we fellowship with God and obey Him, we reflect His nature and become models of His love to our family.

A Proverbs 31 warrior excels because she understands her unique assignment and seeks to do God's will. To excel in life, we must prioritize what God is telling us to do over doing what seems good to do. We may do well when we do good. However, we can only excel when we are in alignment with God's will and purpose for our lives.

Consider this scripture:

Do you not know that those who run in a race all run, but one receives the prize? Run in such a way that you may obtain it. **1 Corinthians 9:24 (NKJV)**

Declare this and pray in tongues: I AM ALWAYS IN ALIGNMENT WITH GOD'S WILL AND PURPOSE FOR MY LIFE.

Intel/Prophetic Insights

Day 48

DAY 49

Charm is deceitful and beauty is passing, But a woman who fears the LORD, she shall be praised.

Proverbs 31:30 (NKJV)

At the end of the chapter, the writer ascribes all that we admire or celebrate about the Proverbs 31 warrior to the Fear of the Lord.

The fear of God is the beginning of wisdom (Proverbs 9:10), and the secret of the Lord is with them that fear him (Psalm 25:14). The fear of God is spiritual intelligence, and it gives access to secrets to success in family life, business, ministry, etc. Through those secrets, we access riches, honor, strong confidence, God's presence in greater dimensions, and the blessed life described in Proverbs 31 (Proverbs 22:4; Psalm 34:9; Proverbs 14:26; Psalm 33:18; Psalm 147:11).

What does fearing God entail?

Proverbs 8:13 (KJV) says, *The fear of the LORD is to hate evil: pride, and arrogancy, and the evil way, and the froward mouth, do I hate.*

How can we become people who fear the Lord? Through a Spirit-empowered relationship with God.

Psalm 34:11 (KJV) says, *"Come, you children, listen to me; I will teach you the fear of the LORD."* The Holy Spirit is our teacher (John 14:26). As we develop a relationship with Him, we begin to love righteousness, hate ungodly ways, and resist every expression of darkness in our realm.

Isaiah 11:2 (KJV) says, *And the Spirit of the LORD will rest on him— the Spirit of wisdom and understanding, the Spirit of counsel and might, the Spirit of knowledge and the fear of the LORD.* Those are dimensions of the manifestation of the Holy Spirit, and it is comforting to know that the Spirit can work in us in a manner that instills the fear of God in us. Glory to God!

Declare this and pray in tongues: I RECEIVE A FRESH BAPTISM WITH THE SPIRIT OF THE FEAR OF THE LORD. THE SPIRIT OF THE FEAR OF THE LORD FINDS EXPRESSION THROUGH ME.

Intel/Prophetic Insights

Day 49

DAY 50

Give her of the fruit of her hands, And let her own works praise her in the gates.

Proverbs 31:31 (NKJV)

God's rewards for seeking Him and prioritizing His agenda are eternal. Eternal rewards begin on earth and continue after the world ends. The elements in the earth, humans, and the realm of the spirit are commanded to yield a fruitful harvest in response to the seeds a Proverbs 31 warrior has sown. All engagements in spiritual warfare, contending for the faith, jealously guarding her relationship with God, and prioritizing the advancement of God's kingdom inside and outside the home, are fruitful.

Isaiah 3:10 (AMP) says, *Say to the righteous that it will go well with them, For they will eat the fruit of their [righteous] actions.* The works of righteousness made possible by grace and the gift of righteousness imputed through the finished works of Jesus produce fruit. God has commanded seed time and harvest, and a Proverbs 31 woman's life will fulfill God's prophecy.

The presence of the Lord within and upon a Proverbs 31 warrior unlocks spiritual gates, granting her recognition in both the spiritual and natural realms. The gates see the King of Glory within her and His glory upon her, and they are lifted up. They acknowledge that a Proverbs 31 warrior carries a weighty dimension of God's presence, bestowed as a reward for yielding to the Spirit of God and doing the works of righteousness.

Read Psalm 24 out loud then pray in tongue:

The earth is the Lord's, and all it contains, The world, and those who dwell in it.

For He has founded it upon the seas And established it upon the rivers.

Who may ascend into the hill of the Lord? And who may stand in His holy place?

He who has clean hands and a pure heart, Who has not lifted up his soul to falsehood And has not sworn deceitfully.

He shall receive a blessing from the Lord And righteousness from the God of his salvation.

This is the generation of those who seek Him, Who seek Your face—even Jacob. Selah.

Lift up your heads, O gates, And be lifted up, O ancient doors, That the King of glory may come in!

Who is the King of glory? The Lord strong and mighty, The Lord mighty in battle.

Lift up your heads, O gates, And lift them up, O ancient doors, That the King of glory may come in!

Who is this King of glory? The Lord of hosts, He is the King of glory. Selah.

(NASB)

Intel/Prophetic Insights

My fellow Proverbs 31 Warrior, let us not grow weary while doing good, for in due season we shall reap if we do not lose heart (Galatians 6:9). I am cheering you on and a great cloud of witnesses is rooting for us (Hebrews 12:1). We are more than conquerors through Jesus Christ!

Continue your Proverbs 31 Warriors adventure by joining the Proverbs 31 Warrior's Community or exploring personalized support.

Scan below for Proverbs 31 Warrior's Community

Scan below for individualized support

About Me

I am on a mission to foster spiritual and emotional intelligence in the family system.

My journey began in the U.S. Army, where I learned the importance of resilience and teamwork. These skills have profoundly shaped my approach to family dynamics. As a Developmental, Individual-Differences, Relationship-based Model (DIR®) practitioner, Certified New Parent Educator (CNPE), and trained postpartum doula, I've gathered a wealth of knowledge to support families during their most transformative moments.

My roles as an author, mom mementor, family coach, speaker, #boymom, and wife are not just titles but reflections of my lived experiences. I understand the unique challenges that parents face, and I am passionate about using research, evidence-based practices, and a heart overflowing with love to guide families towards a life centered on God's Word.

I enjoy conducting research, traveling, educating families, and spending quality time with my family in Georgia. I believe that we most likely share common values and experiences, and I am excited to connect with you.

Made in the USA
Columbia, SC
23 January 2025

44282764-92e4-44a8-b844-ff11e3342321R01